Brandon Lattu
Selected Works
1996–2002

Leo Koenig Inc. New York

Beacon, 1996
gelatin silver print
10 × 8 inches

A black and white photograph of the artist using an antiquated lantern to signal to a late twentieth century city.

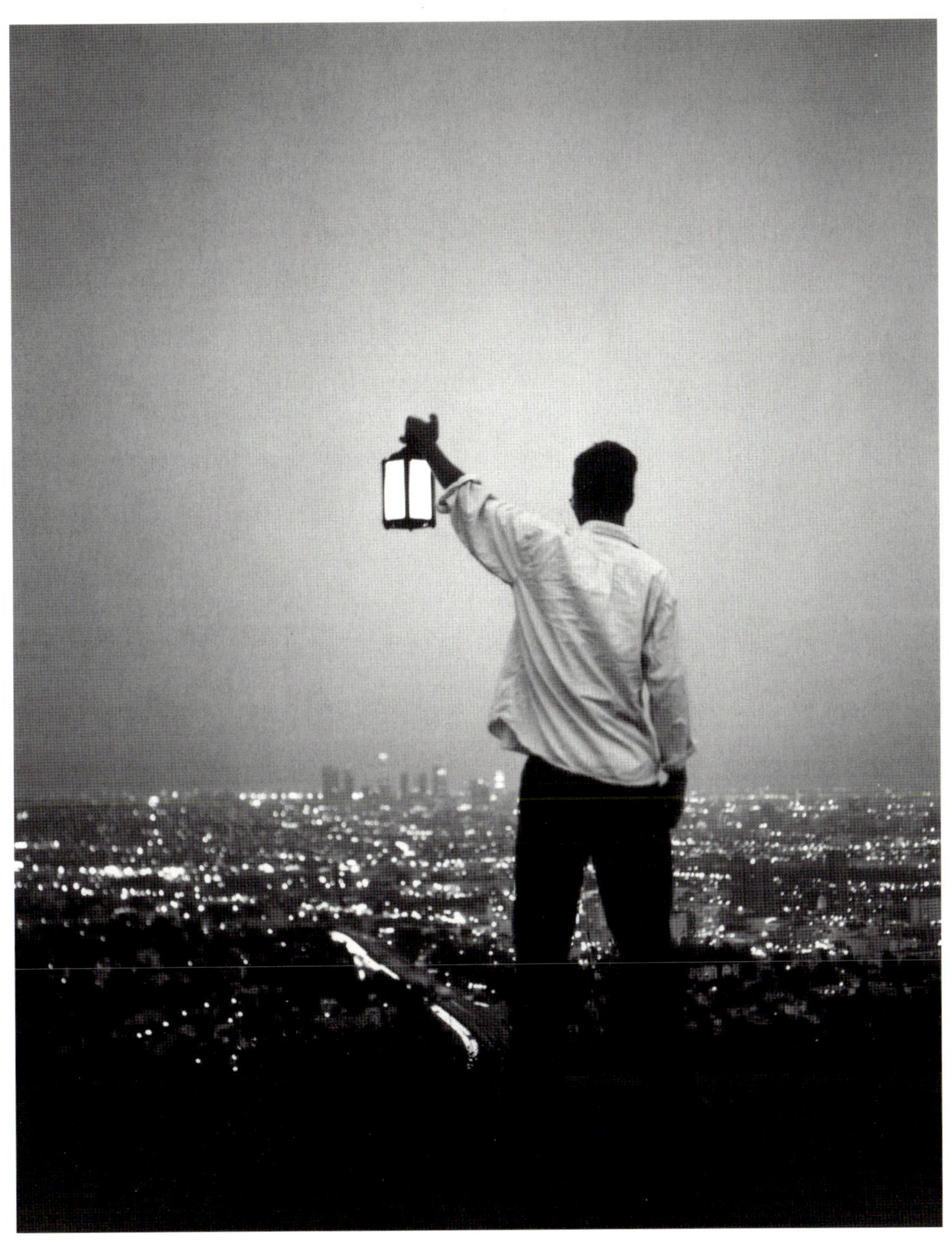

Swarm, 1996
color photograph
5 × 7 inches

Thirty-three airplanes and helicopters photographed in Manhattan during the summer of 1996, montaged into one photograph of the sky over New York City.

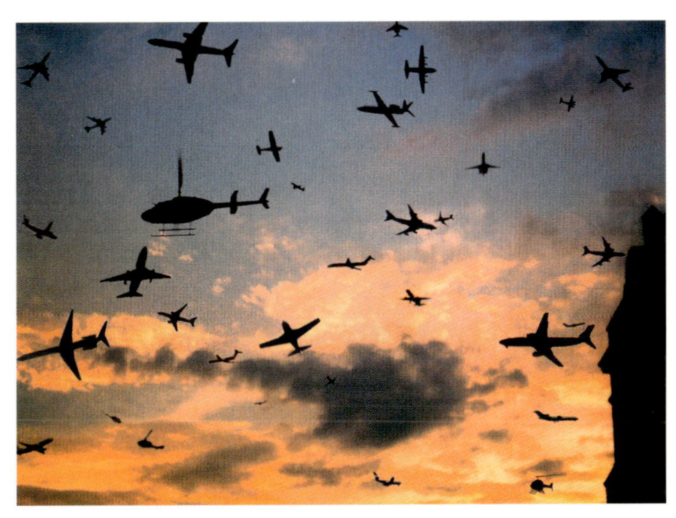

Venetian Ceiling, 1997
color photograph in shaped frame
27 × 40 inches

Fifteen photographs of the ceiling were made from evenly spaced vantage points on the floor. Seamed together, these display the plaster ceiling decoration in an irregularly shaped room in a Venetian hotel.

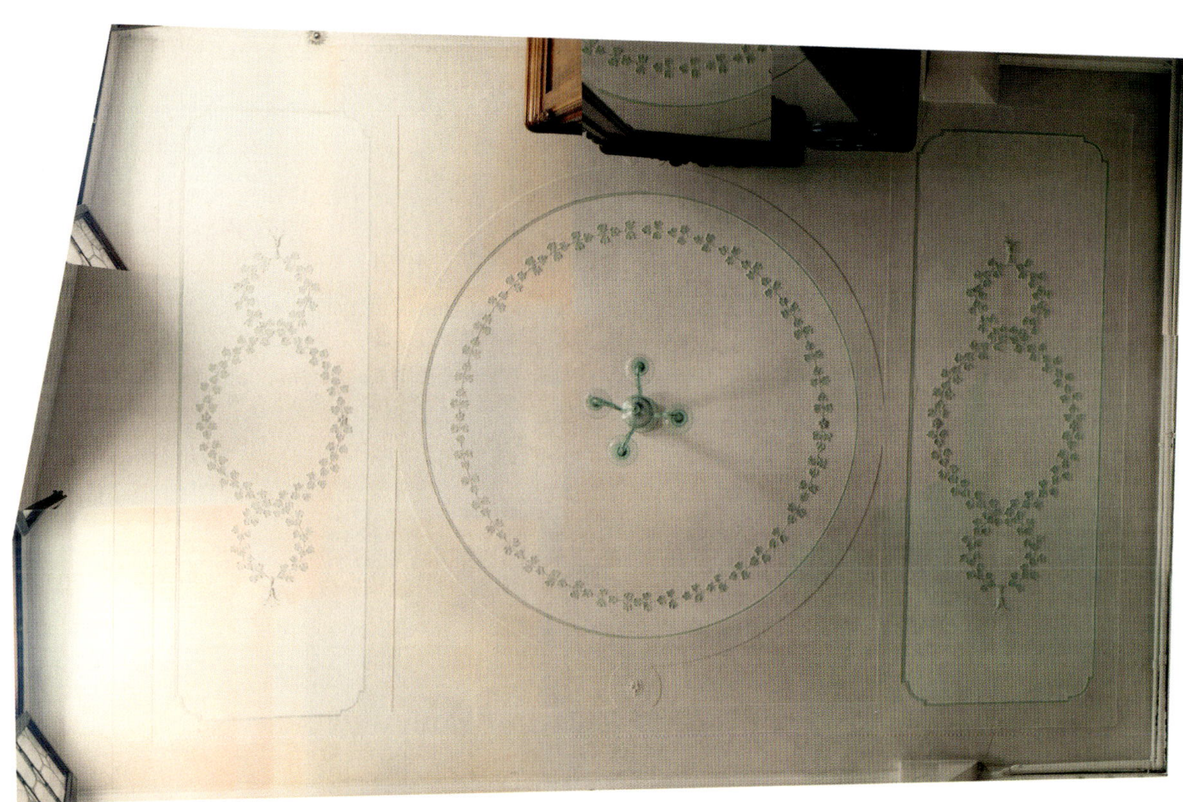

Upstairs and Downstairs, 1997
color photograph
60 × 40 inches

Two photographs presented as one.
Three people in their late twenties living above
the elderly owner of the building, below.
The upstairs photograph was made with the
camera directly against the floor, the downstairs
photograph with it against the ceiling.

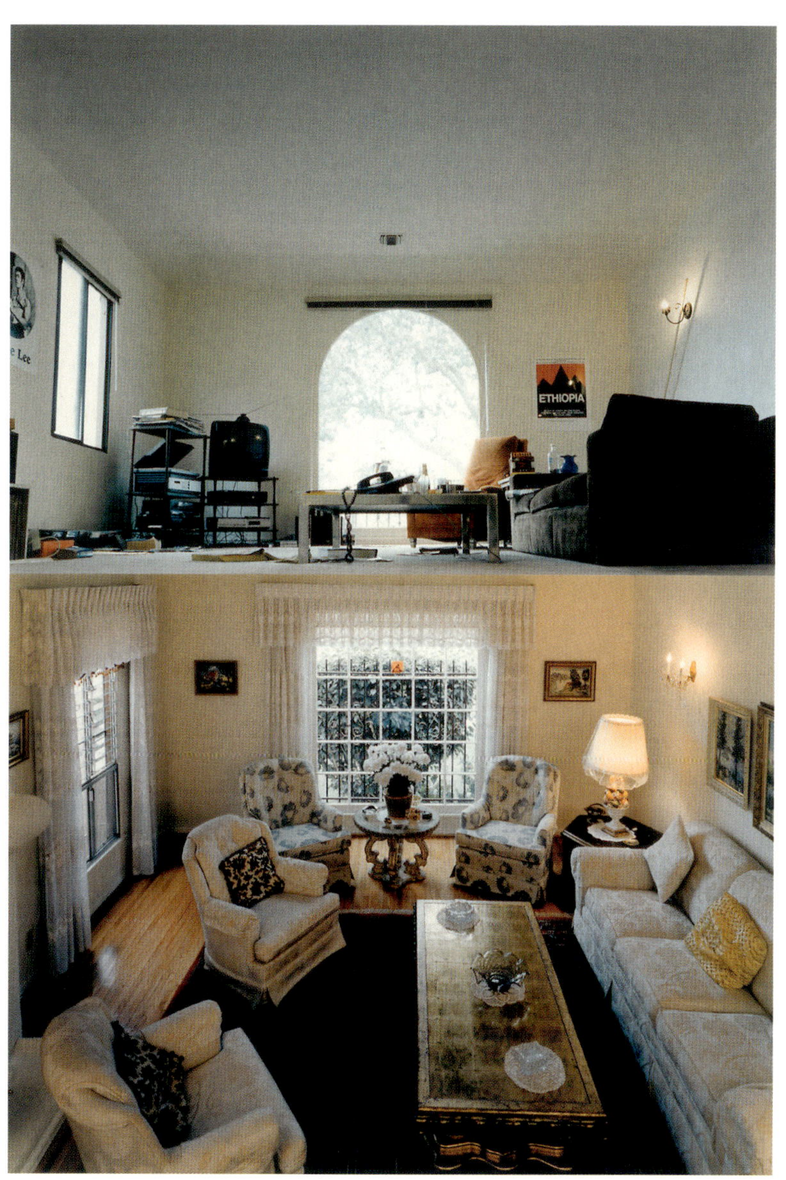
ETHIOPIA

House Projection, 1997
installation of thirty color photographs of varying sizes on acrylic paint on drywall
gallery is constructed of four eight-foot walls arranged to make a twelve by eighteen foot room with a small open doorway

This installation displays two aspects of a three-story house. These aspects are: photographs of the view looking directly out each window in the house, and black painted elevations of each face of the house.
Both the photographs and the elevations are produced at one-quarter scale. In this way, a thirty-two foot tall house is presented in a small room.

Each gallery wall has an elevation of a corresponding face of the original house painted on it. Photographs have been mounted on these elevations in the locations of the original windows, according to plans used to construct the house. The photographs show the view looking directly out the window onto the surrounding landscape as well as anything placed at the plane of the window (such as window treatment or decorative objects).

This installation documentation shows the south, west, north, and east faces of the house; these views are shown clockwise from the top left.

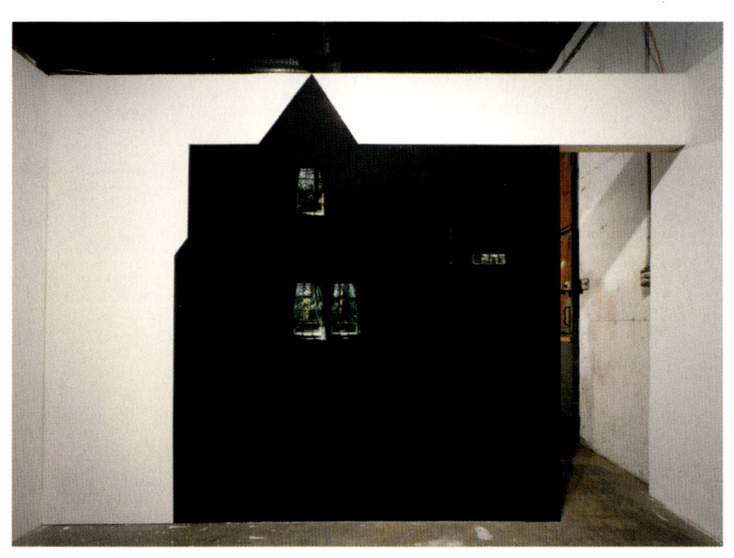
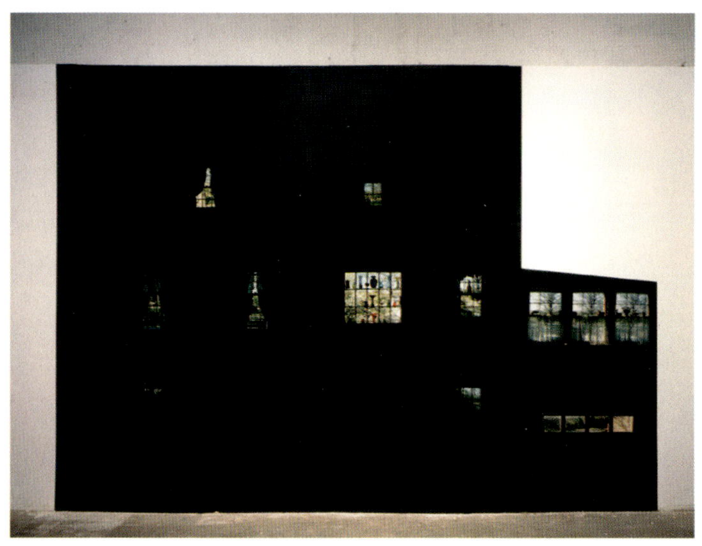
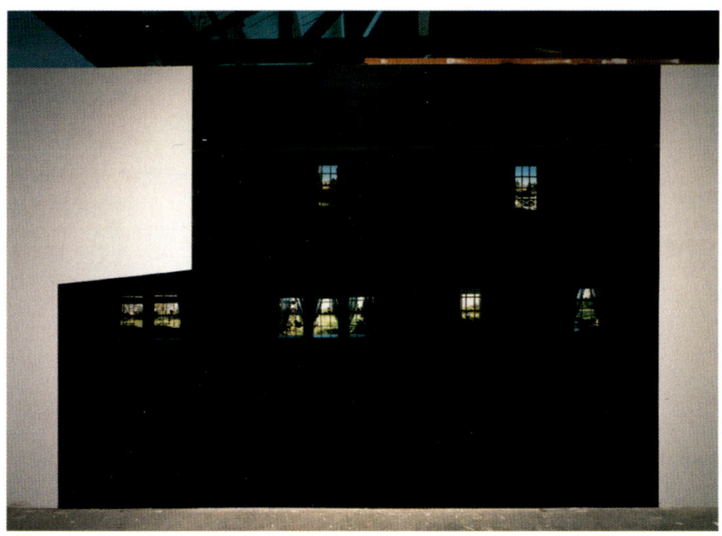
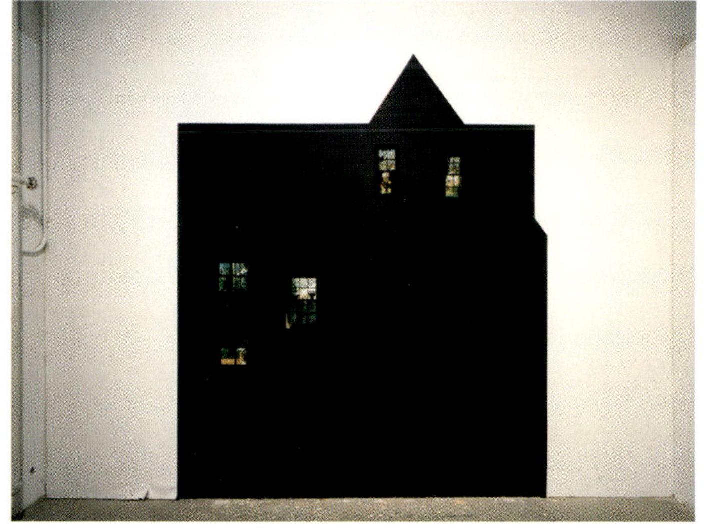

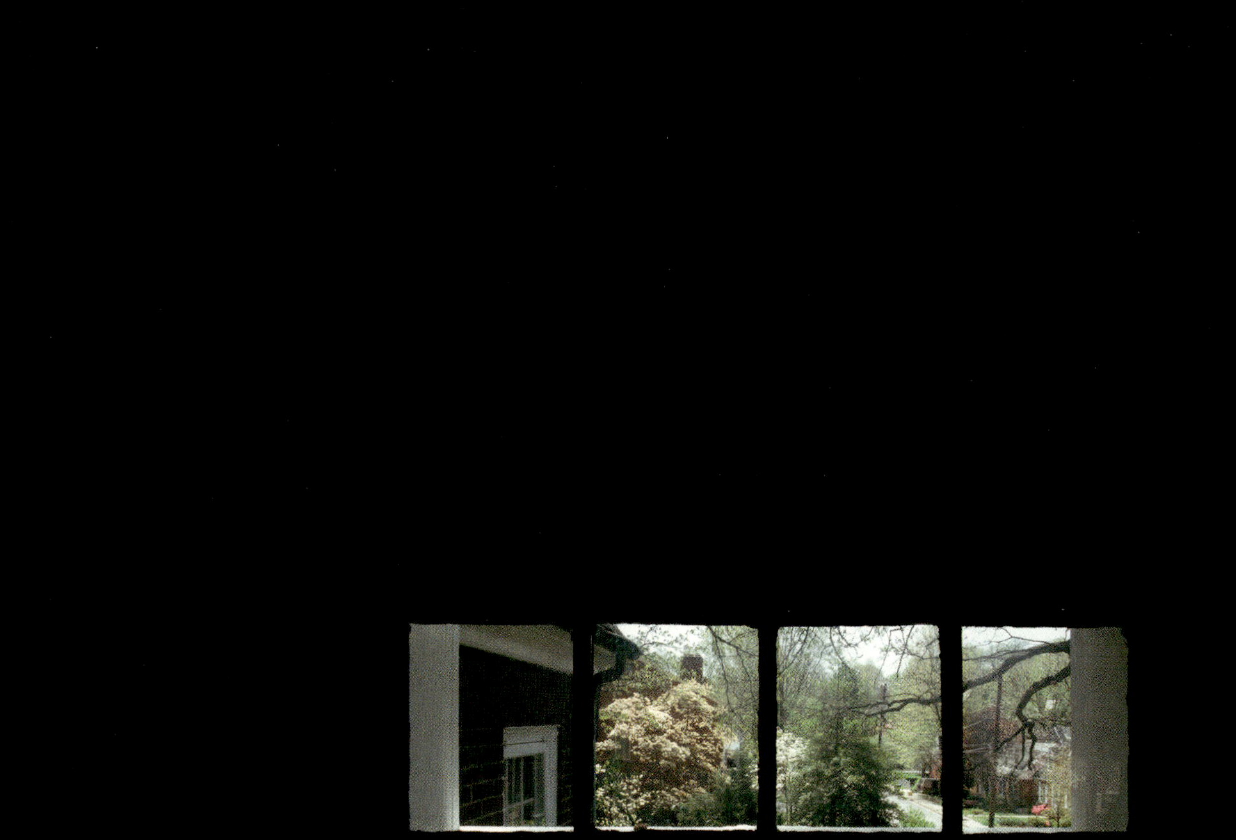

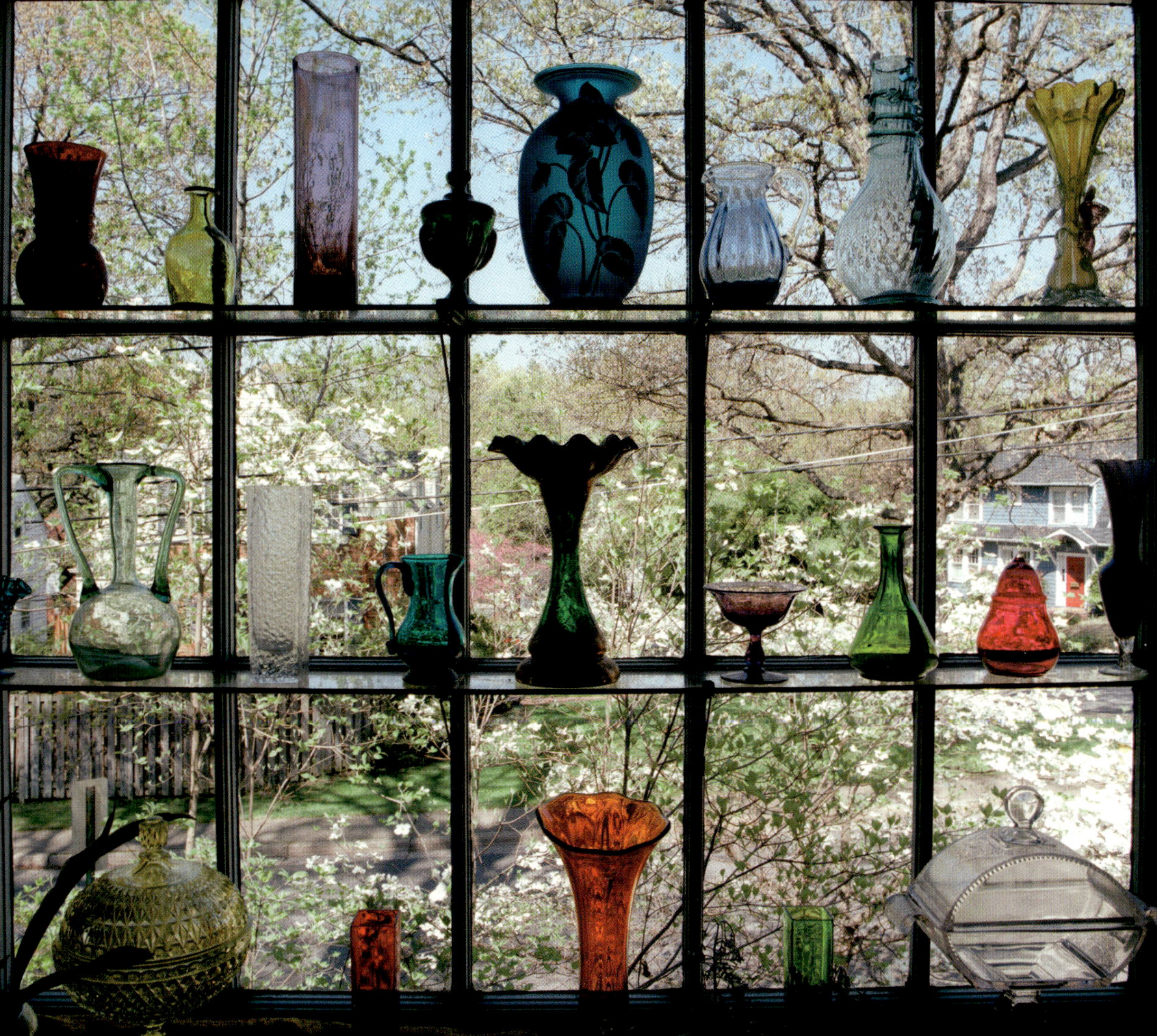

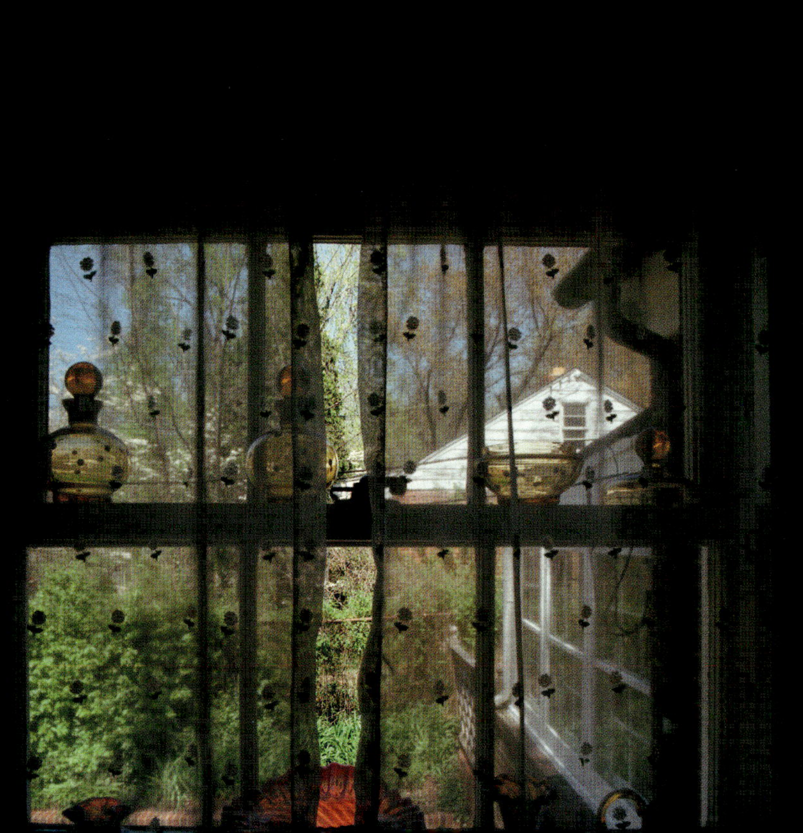

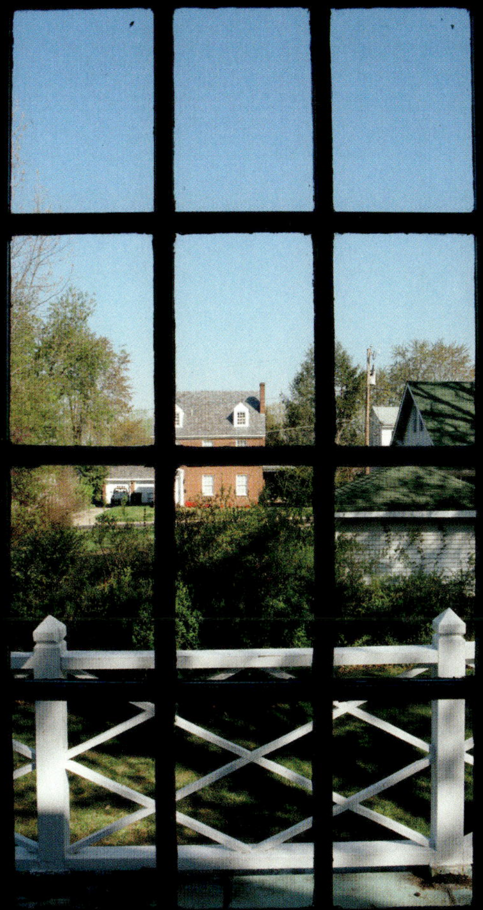

window onto balcony in east wall

Water Under the Bridge, 1998
two channel video installation
floor to ceiling projection

A two channel continuous loop depicting the Merced River's arrival in Yosemite Valley. The projections are stacked and the bottom image has been filmed upside-down. Each channel shows a fixed view looking down at the river from a small bridge. Only the metal barrier rails and the concrete edges of the bridge are shown.
The water progresses up the wall from the rapids at the bottom, through the rails, and then continues downstream, slowing as it reaches the top of the wall.
The end of the loop fades back to the beginning, becoming invisible in the continuous rush of water.

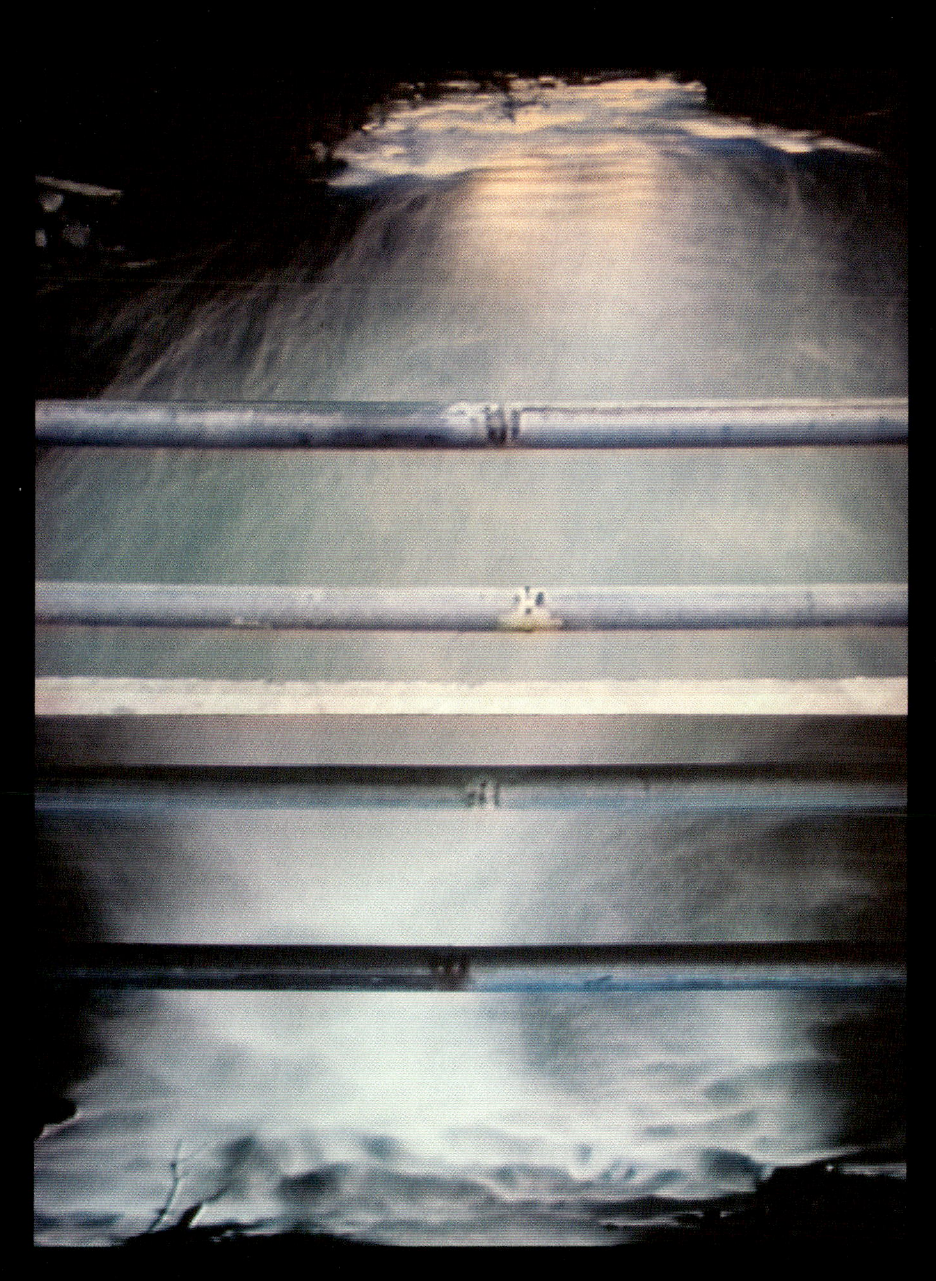

Flat, 1998
color photograph
70 × 90 inches

Each room in an apartment was painted a color specific to its use. During a period of two weeks in June 1997 all of the ceilings were photographed with the camera pointed upwards from the floor. These photographs were scanned at high resolution to depict all the detail of the ceilings (paint texture, dents, etc.) All of the forty-four scans were then montaged together to produce an image of the complete ceiling without perspective. The image is printed at a size (approximately six by eight feet) sufficient to present a picture of a lived-in space in direct relation to the body of the viewer.

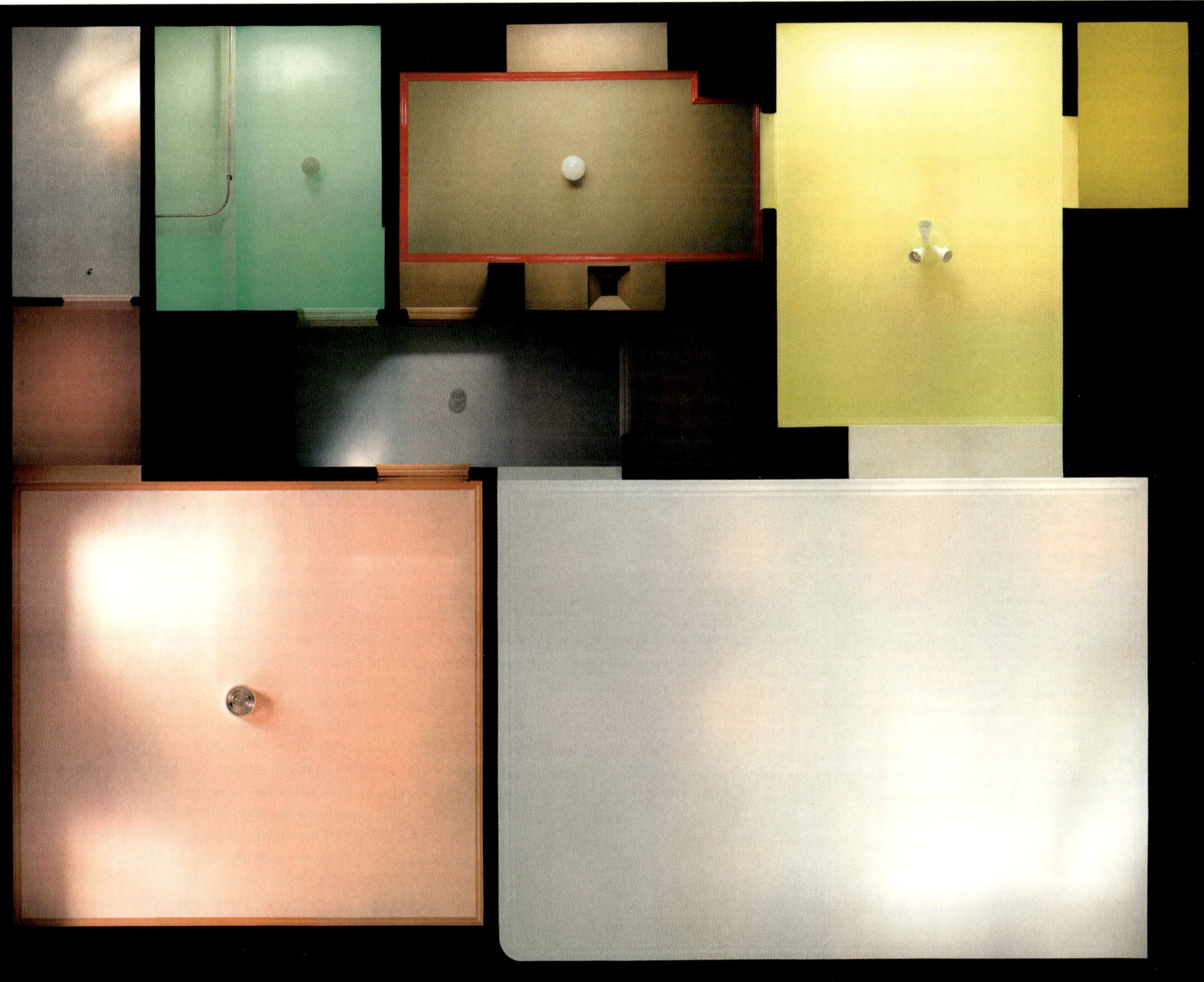

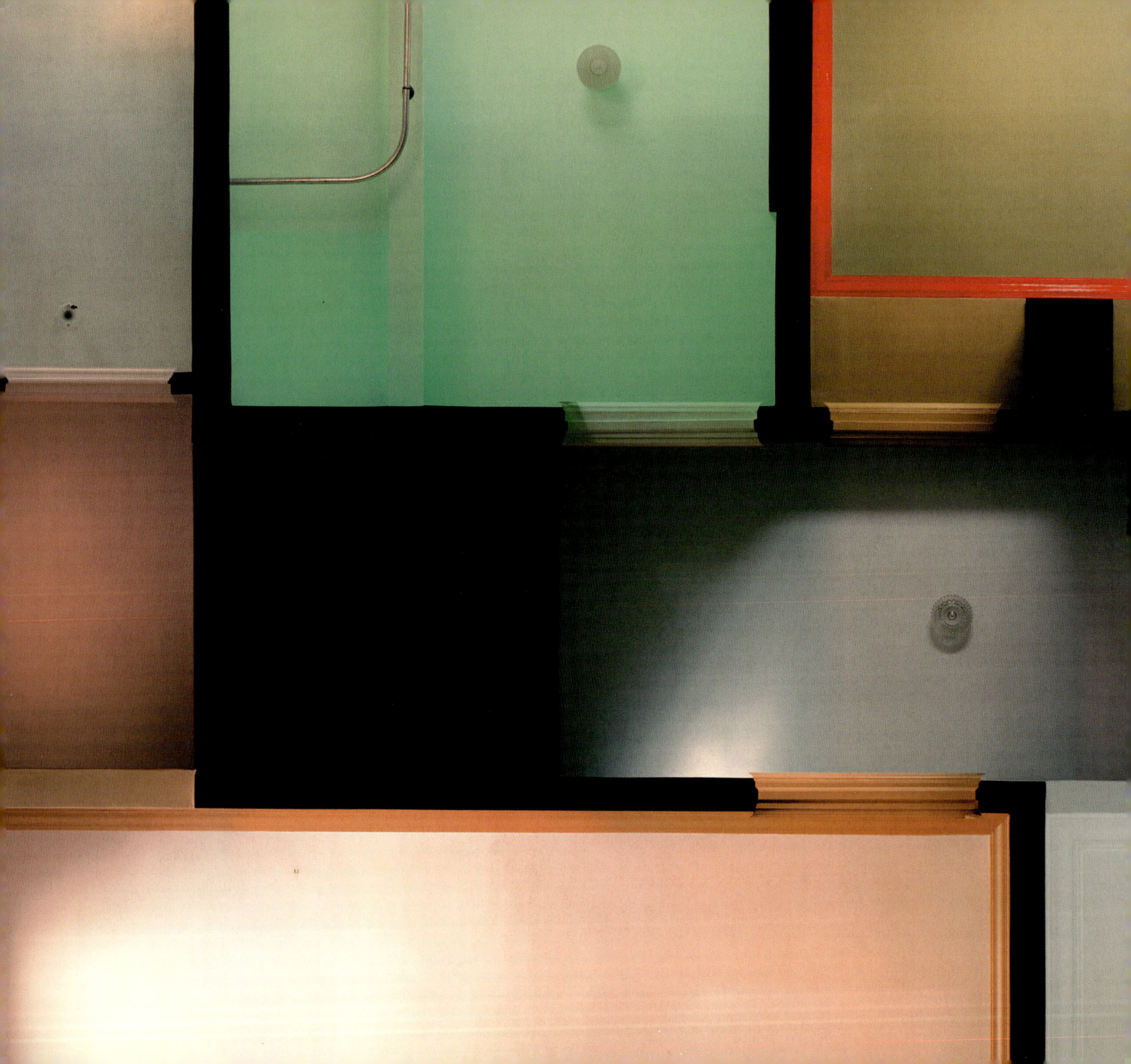

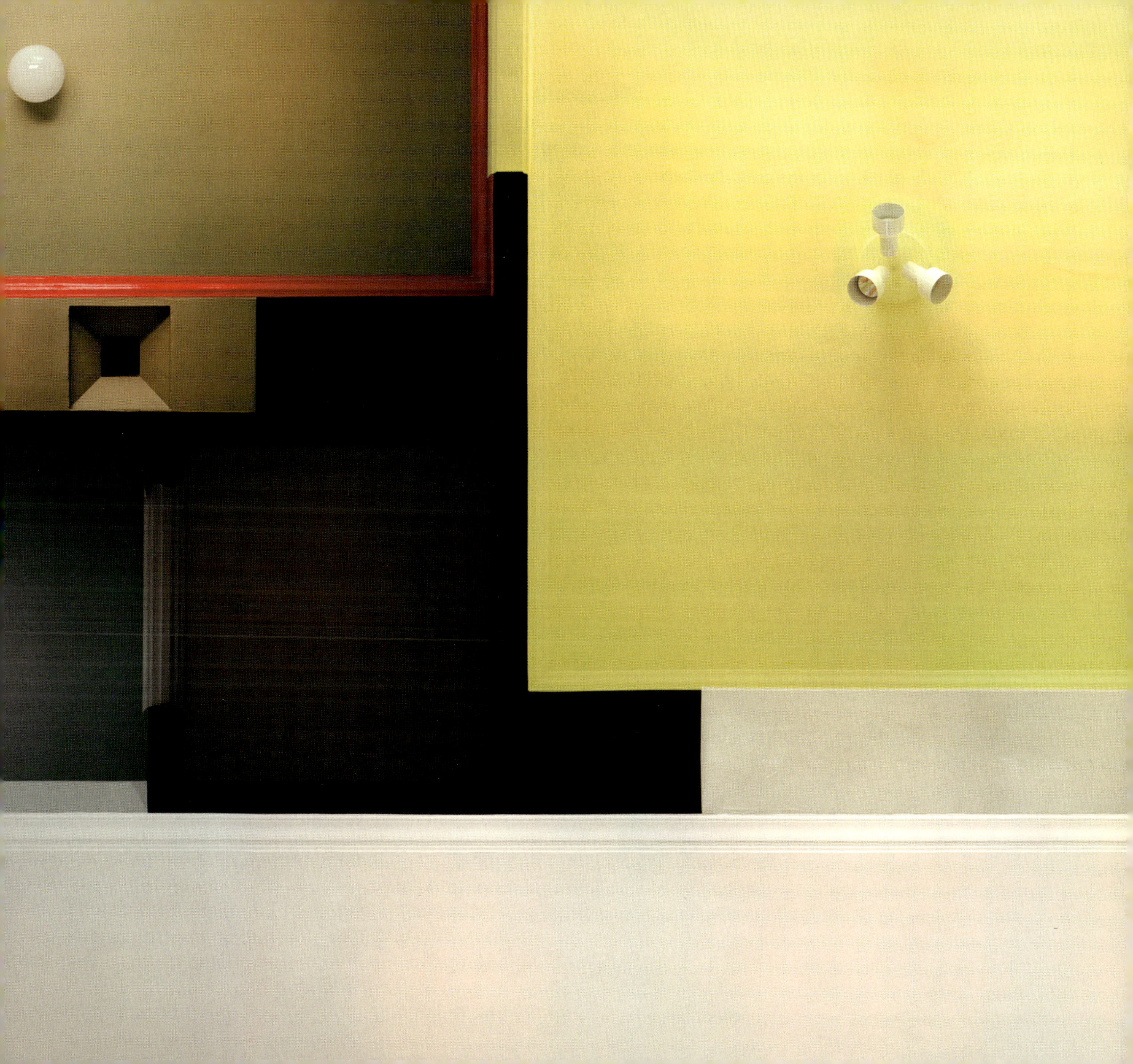

Building Obscured by Signs, 1999
color photograph
9 × 13 inches

This is a conventional 35mm photograph made without alteration of the scene as it was found. The building shown is located near the top of a slight rise, on the north side of 8th Street, in the Koreatown section of Los Angeles.

When shown in group exhibitions, this image is accompanied by an identically framed photograph by Walker Evans titled *Houses and Billboards in Atlanta* from 1936. Evans' photograph was produced under the auspices of the Farm Security Administration and hence exists in the public domain.

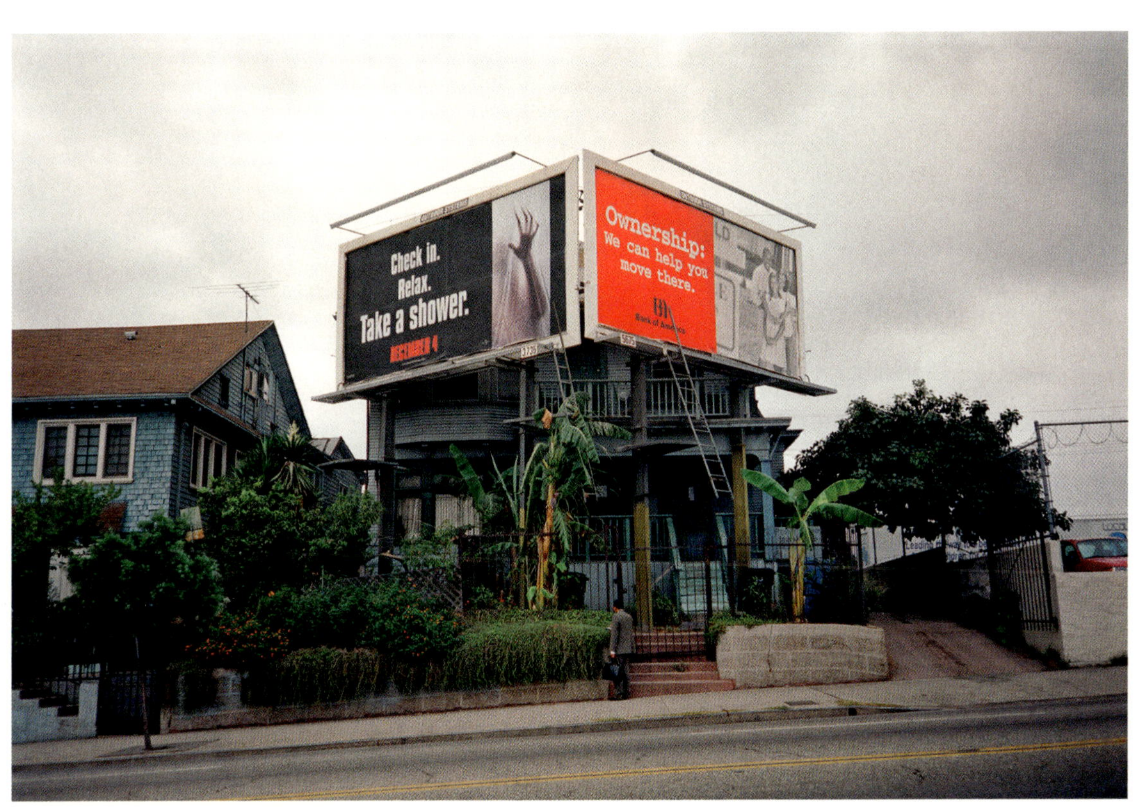
Check in.
Relax.
Take a shower.
Ownership:
We can help you
move there.

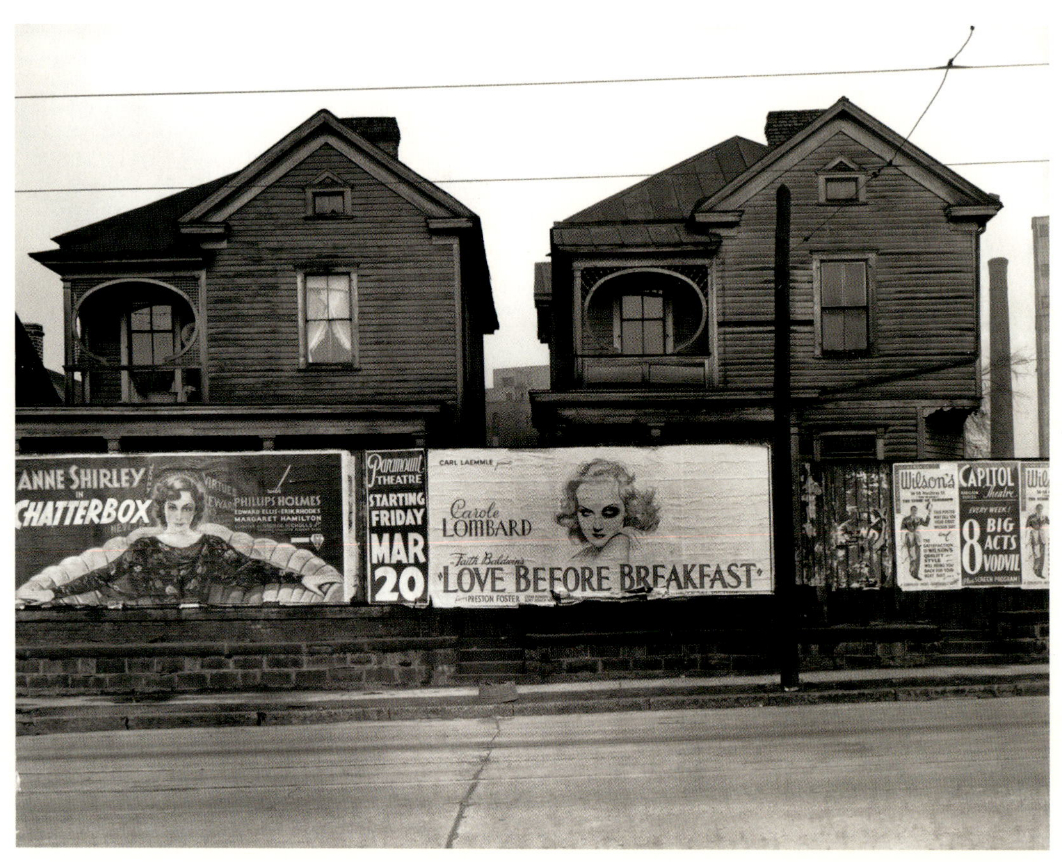

Walker Evans' photograph, *Houses and Billboards in Atlanta* (1936), to accompany *Building Obscured by Signs* in group exhibitions.

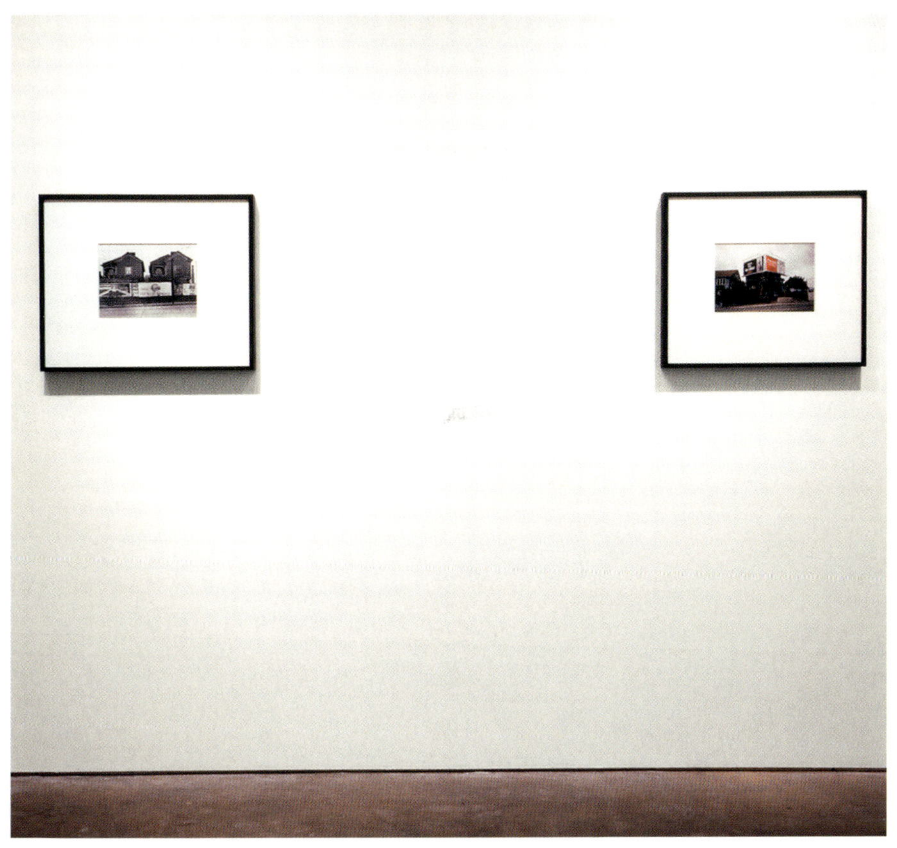

Installation view (from "Zeug Gebrauch Zuhänden",
The Happy Lion, Los Angeles, 2002)

Array, 1999
cyan, yellow, and magenta mylar, tape, and monofilament
dimensions variable
as shown: 35 × 21 × 7 inches, bottom face of cubes at 8 feet from floor

Each cube is made of six faces of cyan, magenta, or yellow mylar. In every case each face has one adjacent face of the same color. Each cube is placed next to another that is either an inversion or a rotation of its pattern. Through this arrangement, the subtractive colors produce the additive colors (red, green, and blue) as the viewer looks through the sculpture. This process is constantly changing as the viewer moves around the space observing the array from beneath.

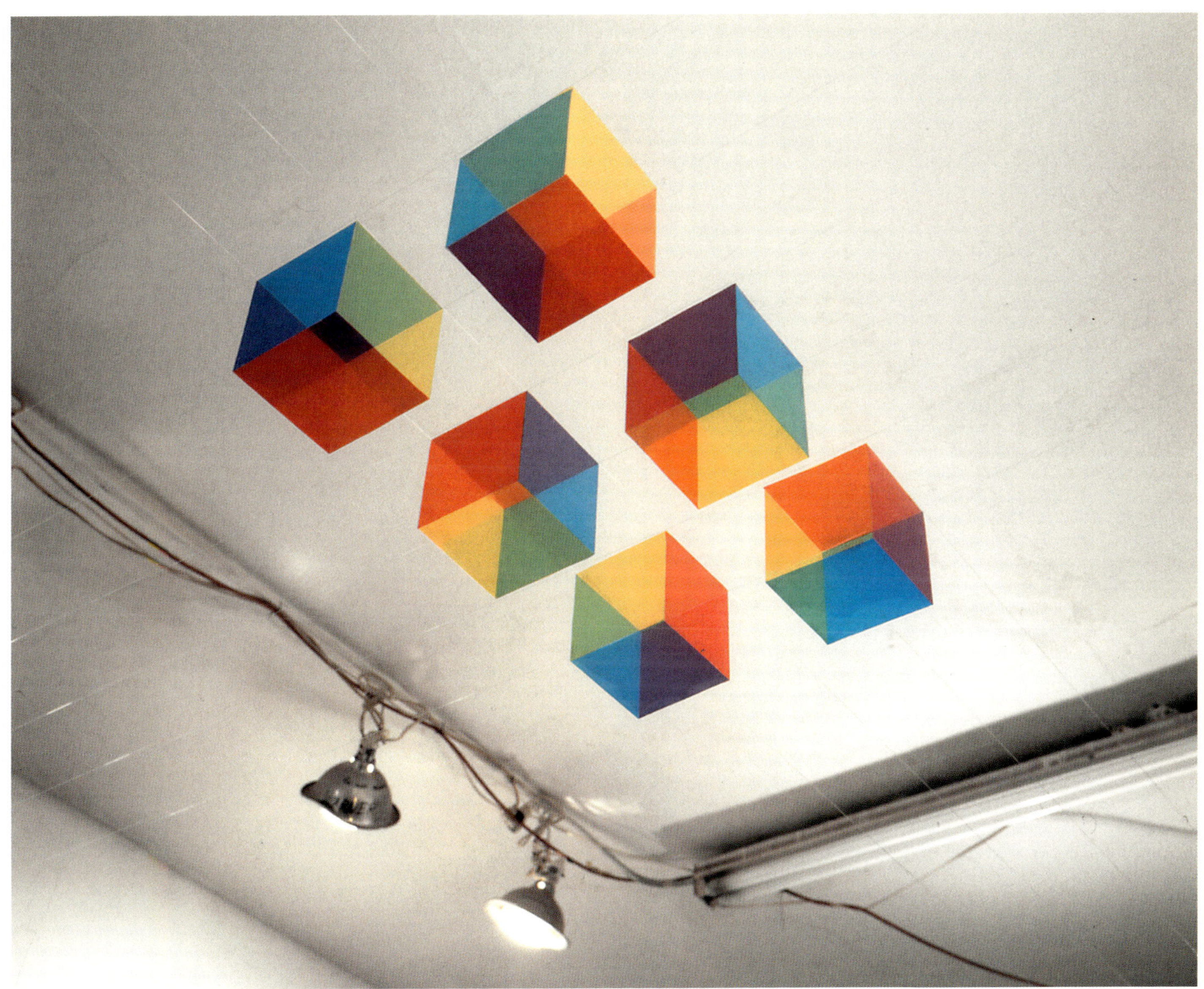

Miracle Mile, 2000
inkjet prints
each 43 × 47 inches

Miracle Mile is the collective title for a group of images depicting internally illuminated signs on Wilshire Boulevard between Fairfax and LaBrea Avenues in Los Angeles. Only signs perpendicular to the flow of traffic on Wilshire are represented. The signs are depicted on a pure black field and no other detail of any form is shown. Every sign is presented in its accurate place and scale relative to the size of the section shown and the scheme as a whole. Because all sizes remain relative, nothing recedes in space as in a perspectival view. In cases where signs read backwards they are facing the opposite direction from the vantage point of the image. When a sign is duplicated for both directions of traffic, only the sign reading correctly for the direction of view is shown.

In this complete view, the area shown is approximately 380 feet high and 420 feet wide (210 feet to either side of the center of Wilshire Boulevard.)

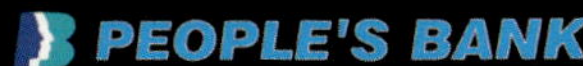

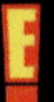

5455

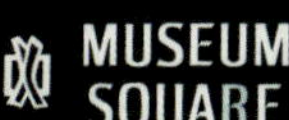

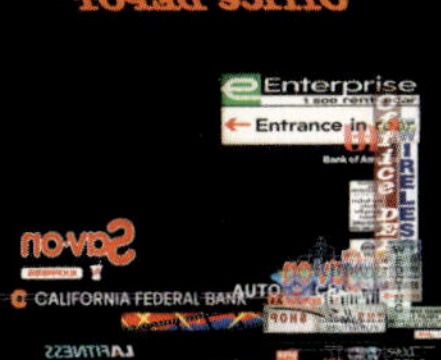

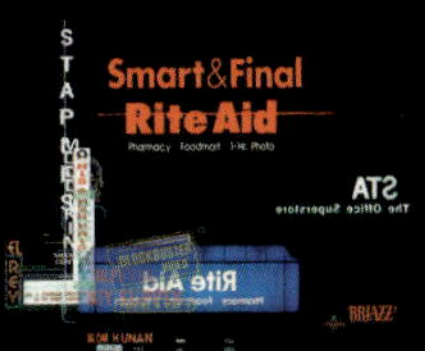

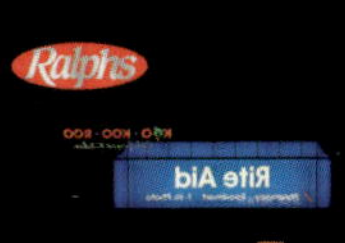

Miracle Mile looking west, skyline view

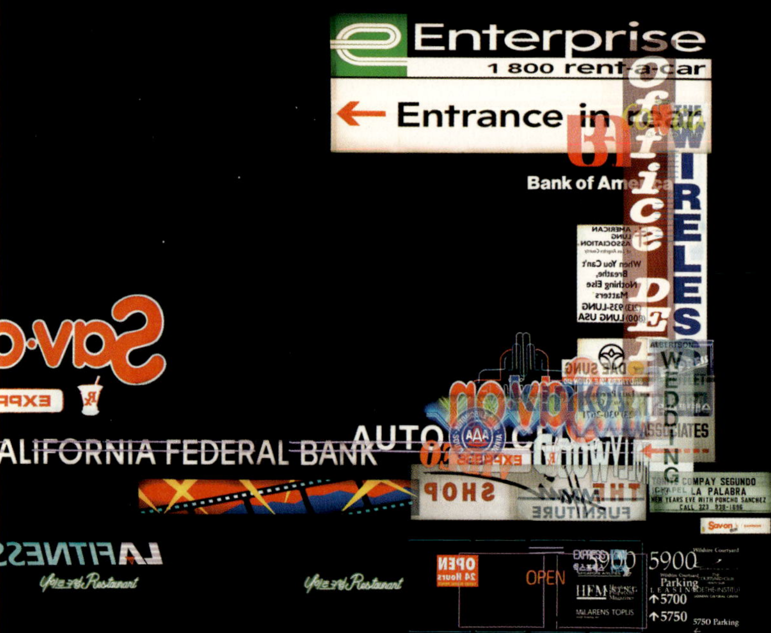

Miracle Mile looking west, south side car view

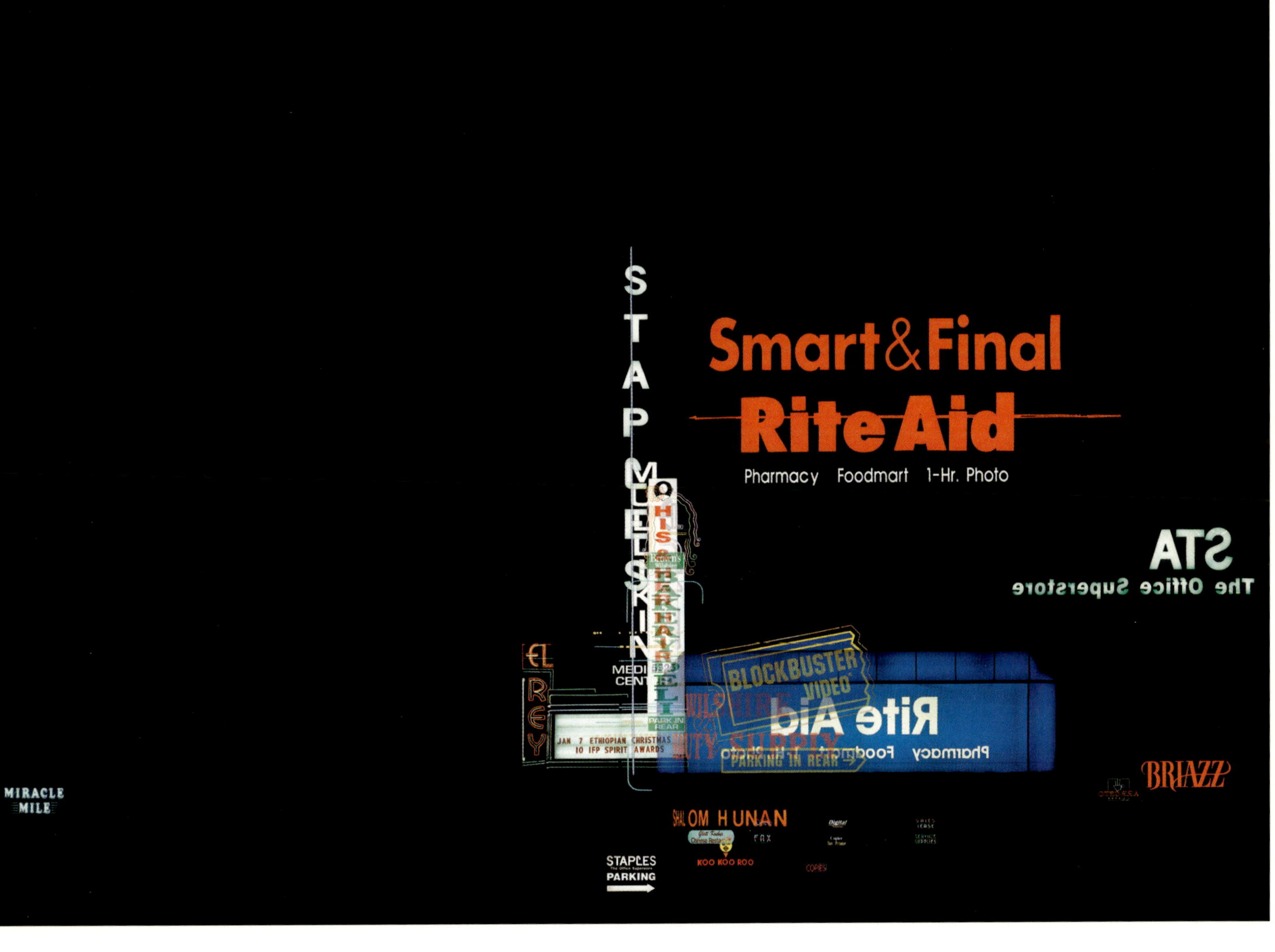

Miracle Mile looking west, north side car view

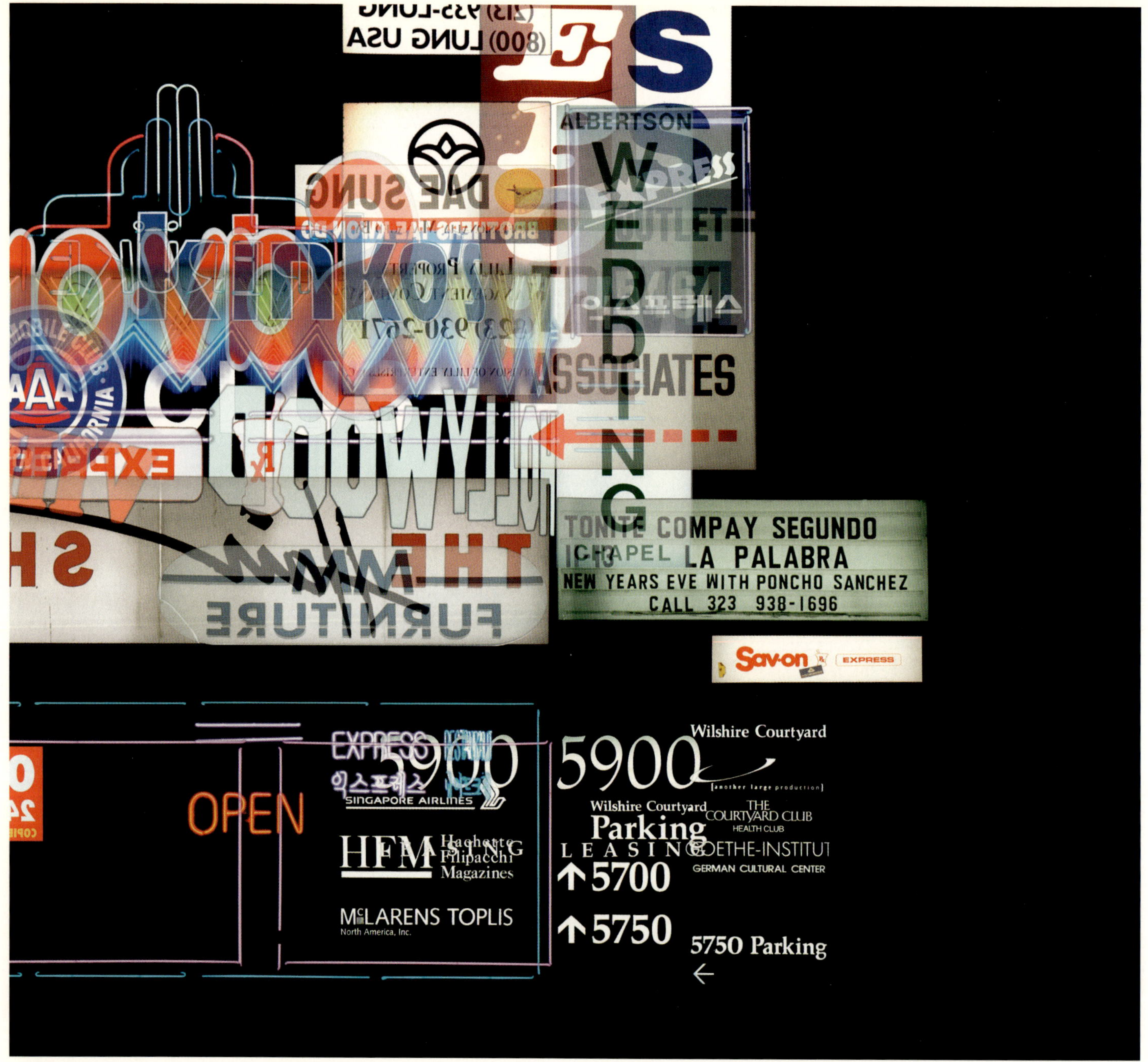

Miracle Mile looking west, south side pedestrian view

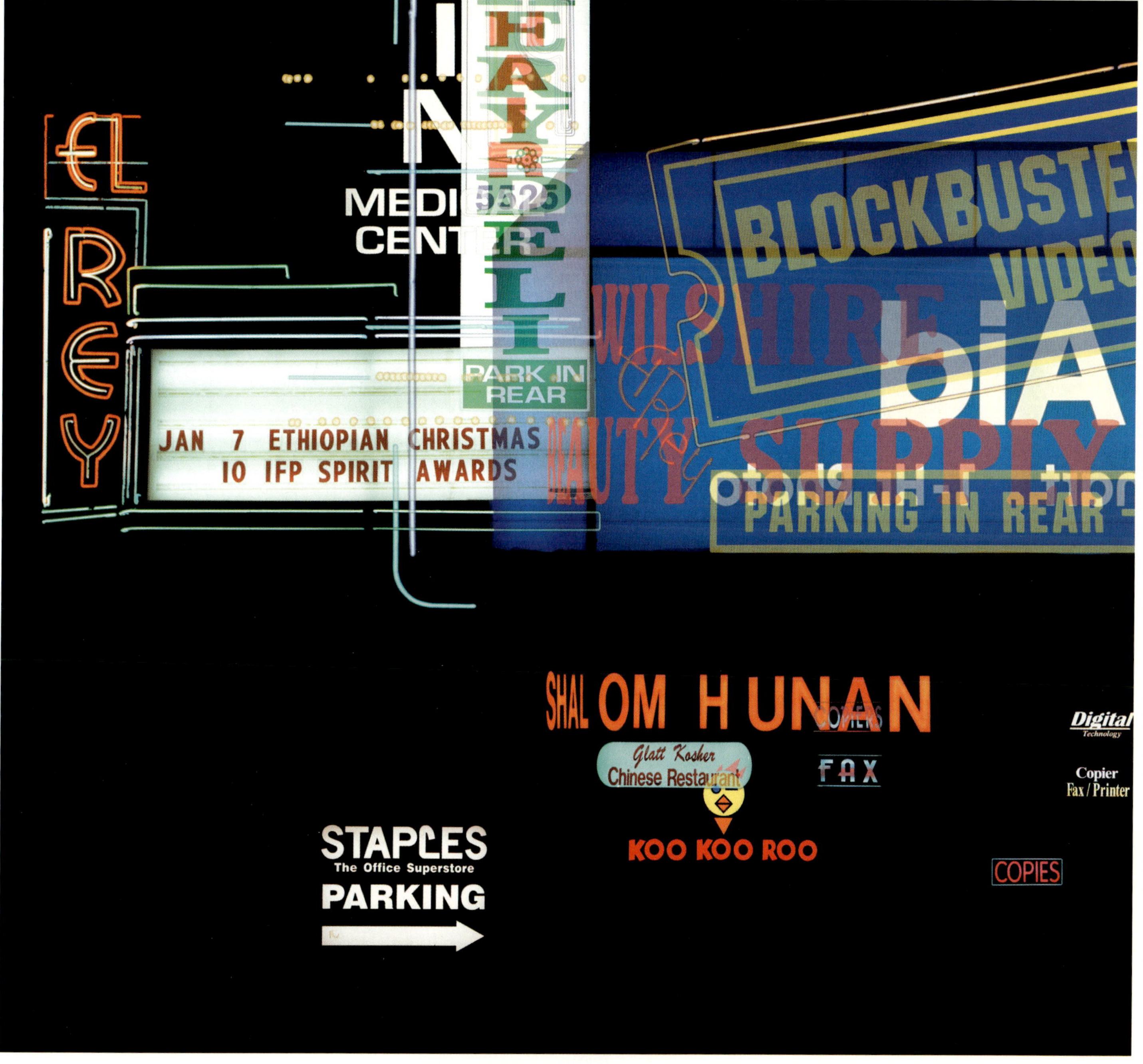

Miracle Mile looking west, north side pedestrian view

Film Without End, 1999–
video on DVD
wall-size projection

Film Without End is an ongoing video project consisting of approximately thirty hours of footage at the date of this publication. The image depicts the landscape passing by the right side of a car while driving at night in Los Angeles. A slide projector next to the video camera in the car projects a white rectangle the shape of a movie screen onto the passing scene. The line of projection (and recording) is about sixty degrees from the direction traveled and angled up slightly to avoid cars traveling in adjacent lanes.

No freeways are recorded, only surface streets that have been traveled previously for reasons unrelated to the production of this video.

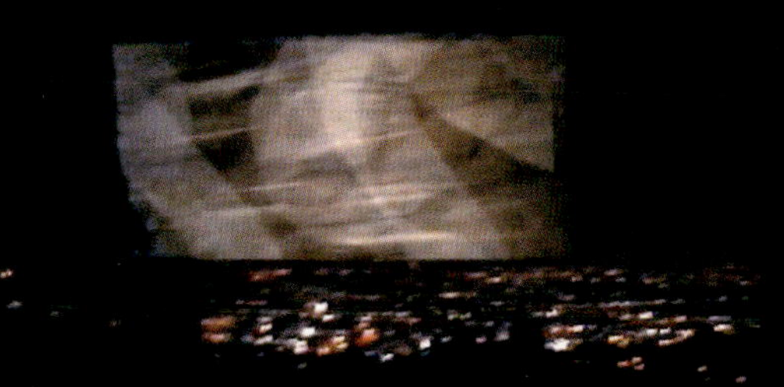

Mulholland Drive, Hollywood Hills

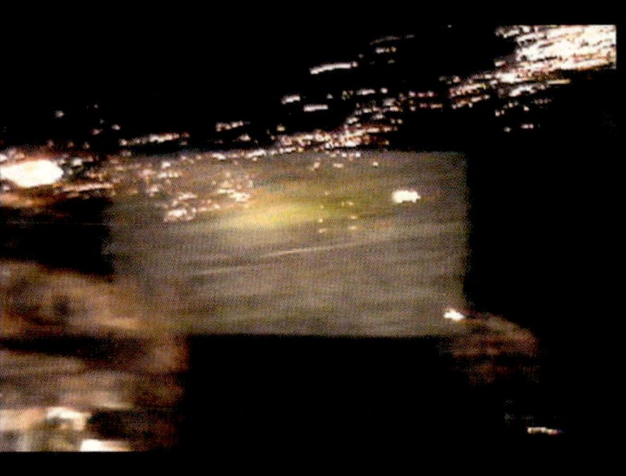

6th Street, Hancock Park

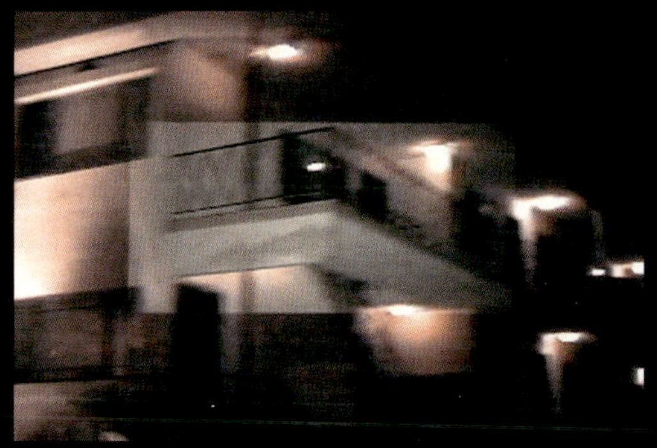

Normandie Ave, Koreatown

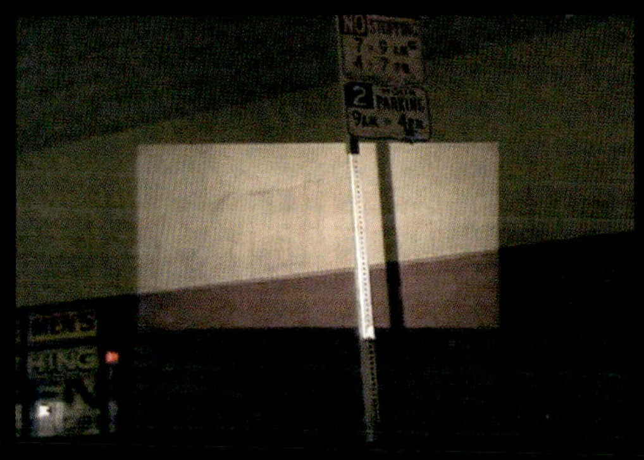

Wilshire Blvd, Miracle Mile

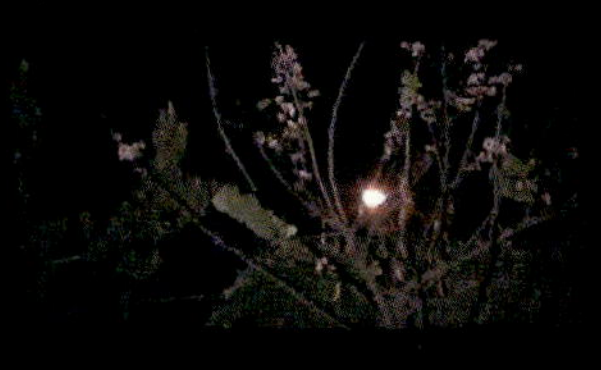

3rd Street, Hancock Park

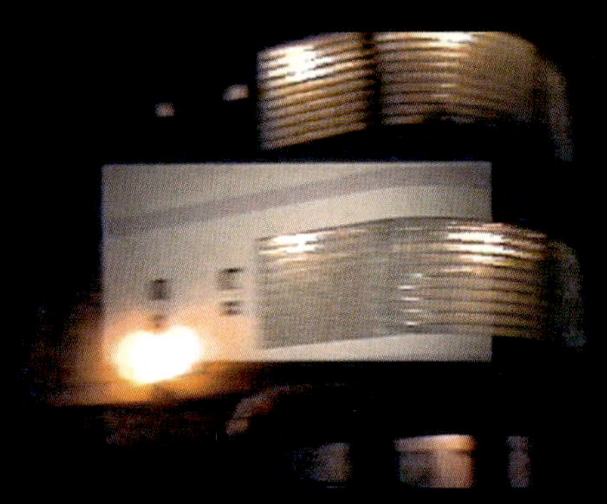

Hauser Blvd, Mid-Wilshire

BARBECUE

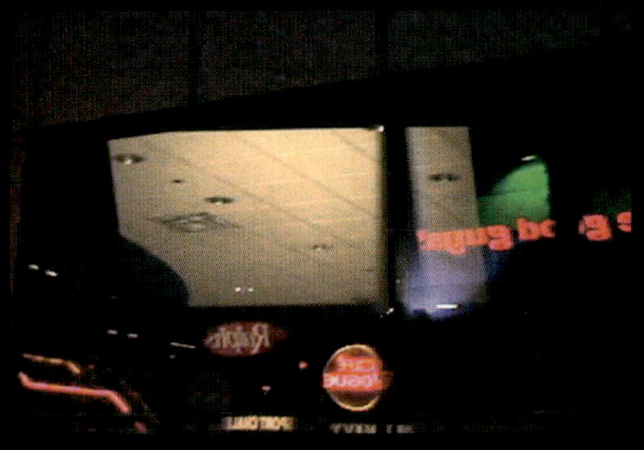

La Cienega Blvd, West Hollywood

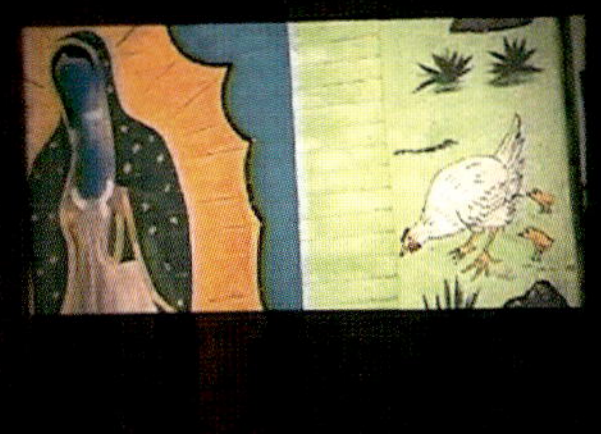

Virgil Blvd, Silver Lake

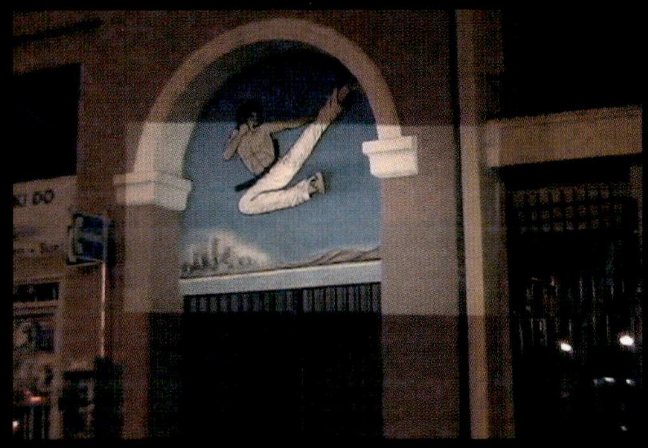

Santa Monica Blvd, Hollywood

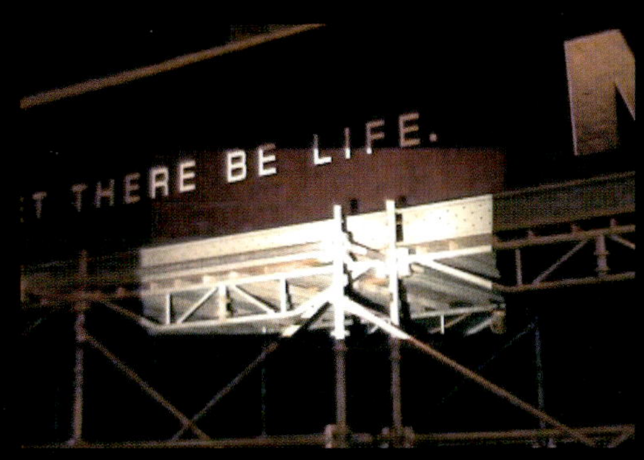

Highland Blvd, Hollywood

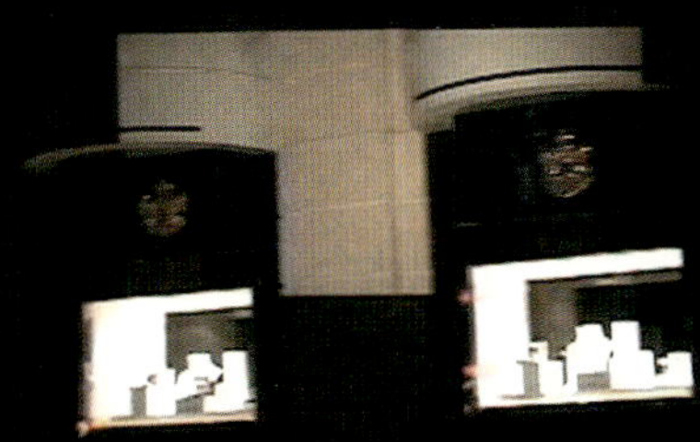

Rodeo Drive, Beverly Hills

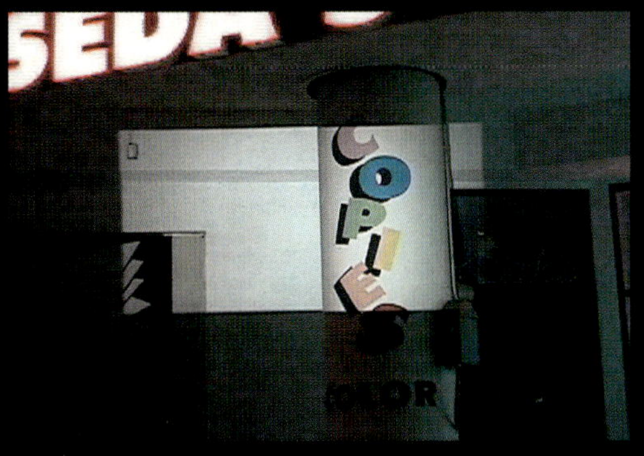

Santa Monica Blvd, Hollywood

Facade, 2001
acrylic mural on temporary wall
11 × 20 feet
Roberts and Tilton, Los Angeles, April 7–28, 2001

Ten motifs from different storefronts found in shopping malls were montaged together and simplified to produce a mural on a wall blocking the street entrance to the gallery.
Glass areas from the original entrances are painted white, while a flat color of paint is chosen to represent all other materials from the original motif.
Daylight coming through the front windows facing the street is visible above the wall.
This photograph (at 11 × 14 inches) of the mural was sold during the exhibition in an unlimited edition.

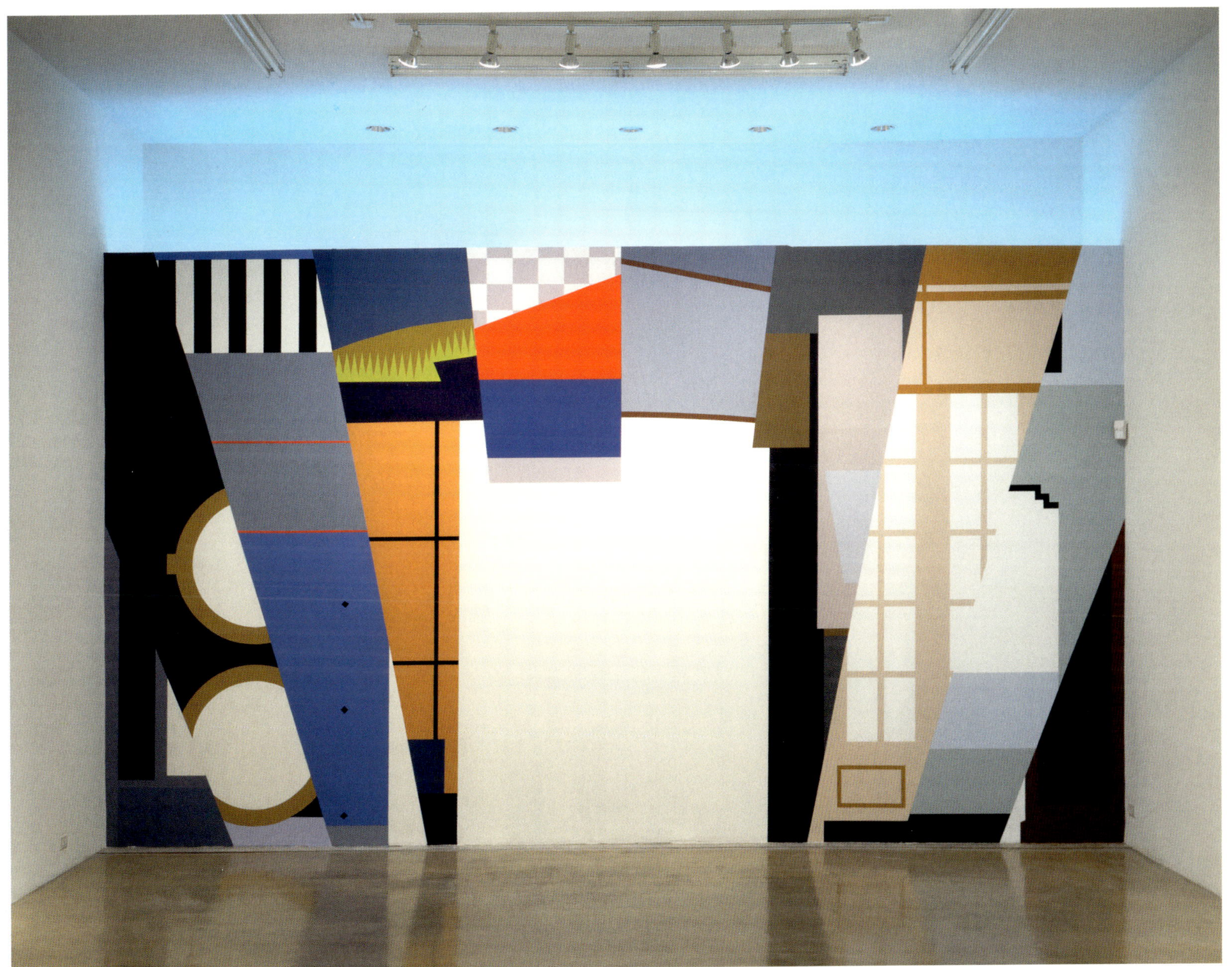

Source montage for *Facade*

The *Facade* mural was produced from this image, a montage of ten different storefronts found in shopping malls in the Los Angeles area. Each section is placed in the same location in the montage as it was in its original storefront.
Stores were chosen as each being representative of a type of commercial decor, with the goal of covering the gamut available.

Stores represented (left to right): Rand McNally Maps, Sunglasses Hut, Foot Locker, PetLove, KayBee Toys, Fox 1hr Photo, Contempo Casual, Victoria's Secret, See's Candy, and Brentano's Books.

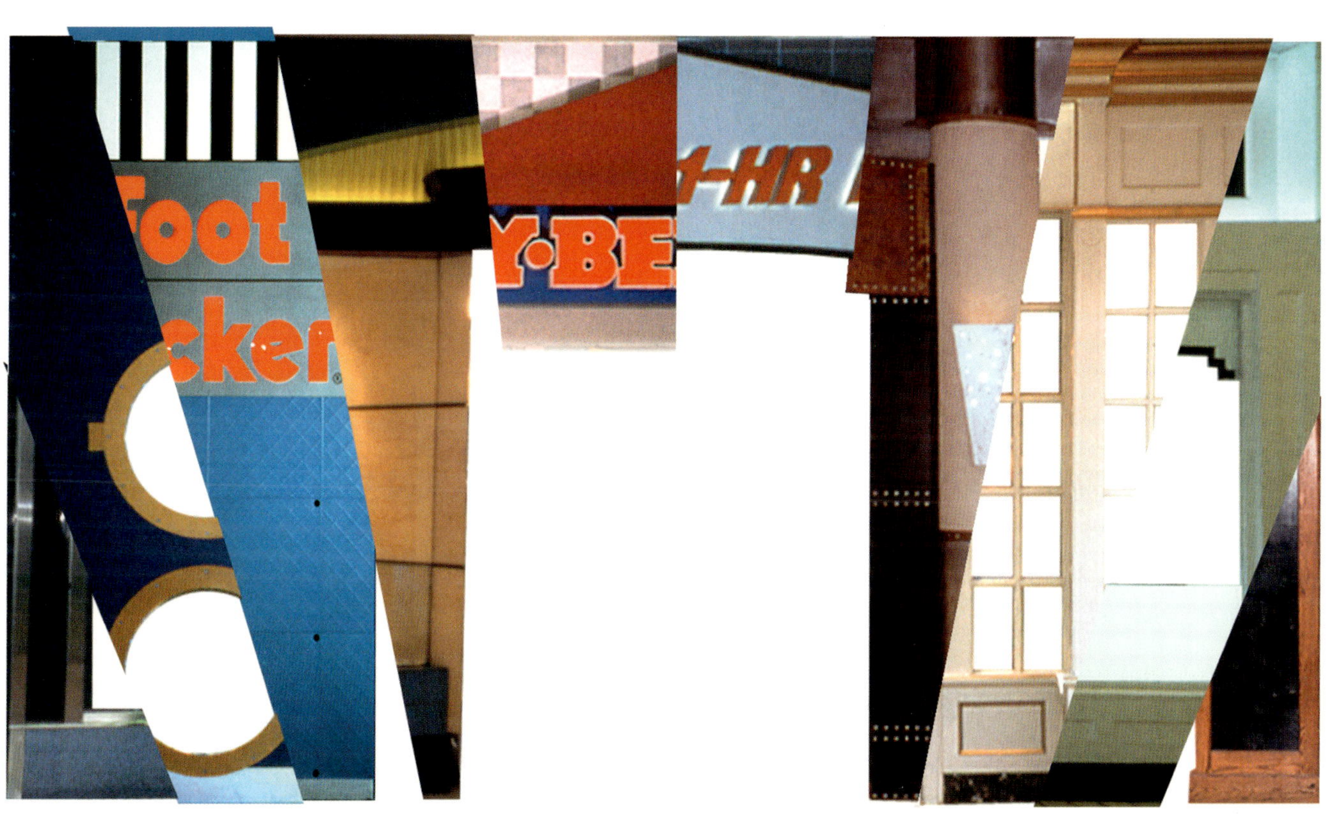
Foot
cker
Y·BE
-HR

Selected Products, 2001
inkjet print
24 × 30 inches

Boxes for consumable products used in my household are arranged and presented as empty and transparent.

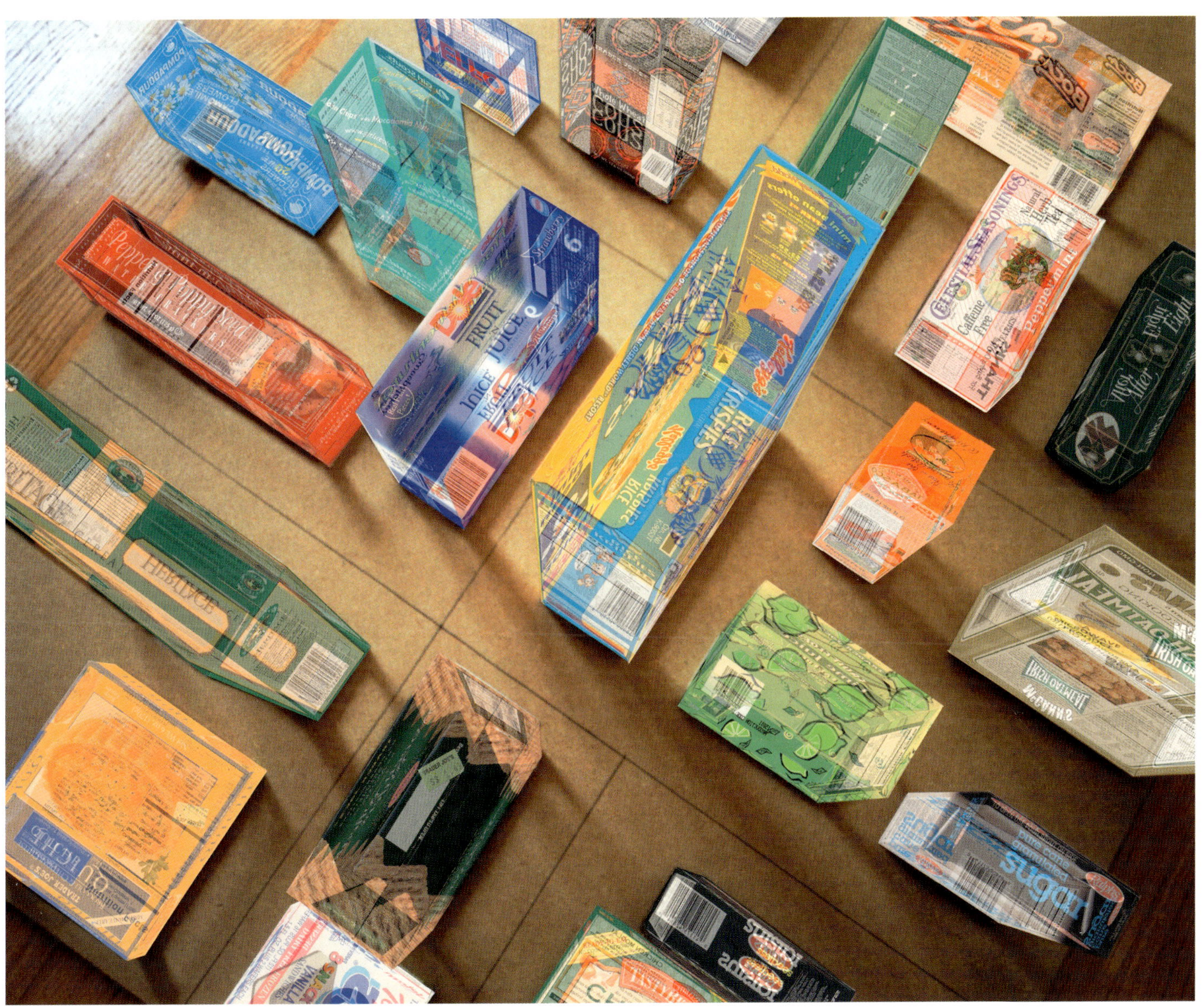

Rejected Products, 2002
inkjet print
24 × 30 inches

Identical to piece of previous year (*Selected Products*) except that equivalent products with different boxes are chosen instead. In most cases these are competing or generic versions; in a few cases they are flavors that we don't like; and in one case the packaging changed in the intervening time.

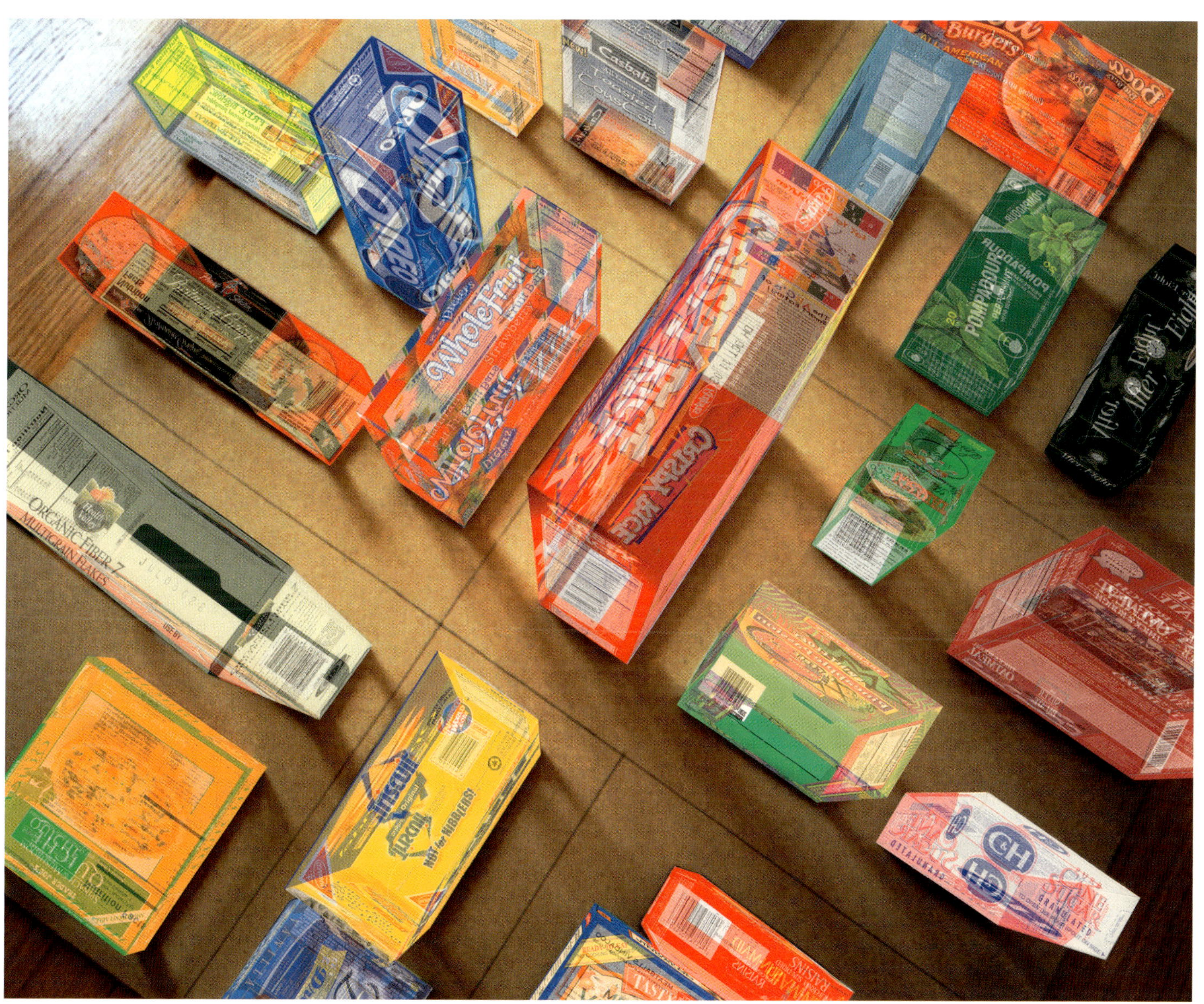

WholeFruit
Strawberry
Casbah
Toasted
CousCous
Burgers
ALL AMERICAN
POMPADOUR
ORGANIC FIBER 7
MULTIGRAIN FLAKES
NOT for NIBBLERS!
C&H
CANE SUGAR
GRANULATED
RAISINS
After Eight

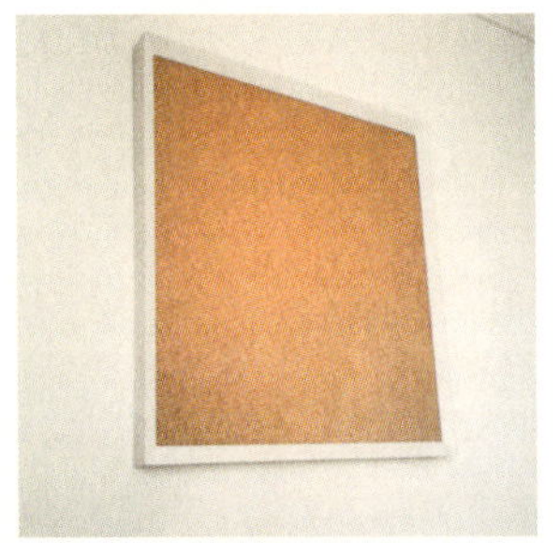

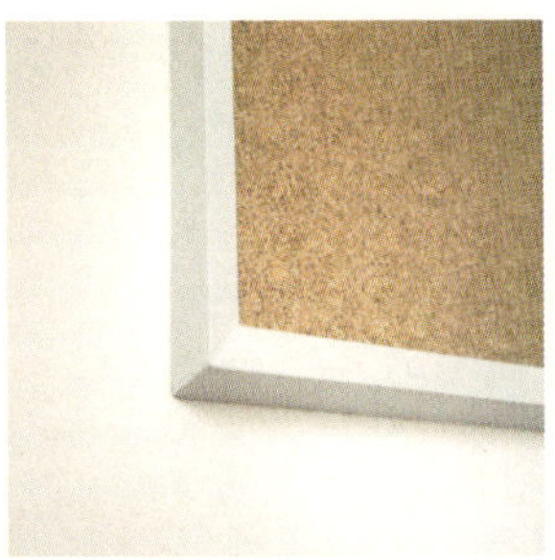

Sand, Point Dume, Malibu, California, 2001
inkjet print in specific frame
20 x 24 inches

Sand was collected from the beach at Point Dume. This sand was scanned at the highest resolution available. The image produced was then printed to make the most faithful rendition of the source material possible.

Detail shown opposite printed actual size.

I would like to thank the following people for their assistance in labor, council, or both for this publication:

Joseph Amodio, Donald Breckenridge, Ken Ehrlich, Silke Fahnert, Morgan Fisher, David Hughes, Allyson Johnson, Uwe Koch, Alison Lattu, Jon Pestoni, Cory Reynolds, Jeremy Sigler, and Amir Zaki. Extra gratitude is due to Uta Barth for her patient advice of all sorts and to Leo Koenig for making this publication possible.

With love, this book is dedicated to Janine Huebner and Sophie Lattu.

BRANDON LATTU

LAYOUT & TYPESETTING: Silke Fahnert, Uwe Koch, Cologne
PRODUCTION: Druckerei Zimmermann, Cologne

DISTRIBUTION (INSIDE EUROPE):
Buchhandlung Walther König, Köln

DISTRIBUTION (OUTSIDE EUROPE):
D.A.P./Distributed Art Publishers, Inc., New York
155 Sixth Avenue, New York, NY 10013
Phone 212-627-1999, Fax 212-627-9484

ISBN: 3-88375-917-1 Printed in Germany

COVER: *Under the Marquee*, 2003

I would like to thank the following people for their assistance in labor, council, or both for this publication:

Joseph Amodio, Donald Breckenridge, Ken Ehrlich, Silke Fahnert, Morgan Fisher, David Hughes, Allyson Johnson, Uwe Koch, Alison Lattu, Jon Pestoni, Cory Reynolds, Jeremy Sigler, and Amir Zaki. Extra gratitude is due to Uta Barth for her patient advice of all sorts and to Leo Koenig for making this publication possible.

With love, this book is dedicated to Janine Huebner and Sophie Lattu.

BRANDON LATTU

LAYOUT & TYPESETTING: Silke Fahnert, Uwe Koch, Cologne
PRODUCTION: Druckerei Zimmermann, Cologne

DISTRIBUTION (INSIDE EUROPE):
Buchhandlung Walther König, Köln

DISTRIBUTION (OUTSIDE EUROPE):
D.A.P./Distributed Art Publishers, Inc., New York
155 Sixth Avenue, New York, NY 10013
Phone 212-627-1999, Fax 212-627-9484

ISBN: 3-88375-917-1 Printed in Germany

COVER: *Under the Marquee*, 2003